The Best Ever
CAKE
BOOK

DK

Banana and pecan cake, page 14

Mixing, page 12

Strawberry shortcakes, page 38

Contents

Celebration cake, page 44

Kitchen rules

Baking is fun! Here is what you'll need to know before you get started. You will need an adult to help you with all the recipes in this book.

KITCHEN SAFETY

Be very careful...

• When you see the warning triangle, take extra care and ask an adult for help.

• Be careful around hot ovens, and gas or electric burners, making sure you know whether the oven or stovetop is on and protecting your hands when **touching or lifting anything hot** from, or on, or into it. **Oven mitts** are your friends here!

• Take extra care when handling hot liquids or hot pans, watching carefully for spills, and protecting your hands (using oven mitts or a dish towel) when moving or holding hot items. Tell an adult immediately if you get a burn.

• Be careful when handling anything sharp, such as knives or a grater. Take extra care when cutting anything with a sharp knife.

• When using power tools, such as food processors and mixers, check if they're on and don't put your hands near the moving parts until you have switched them off at the socket.

IF IN DOUBT ask an ADULT to help, especially when you're unsure about anything.

INGREDIENTS AND EQUIPMENT

• Make sure you have all your ingredients laid out before you start to make a recipe. You'll probably have most ingredients in your kitchen already, but some you will need to buy.

• Always use the type of flour specified in a recipe—bread, all-purpose, or self-rising.

• Use medium-sized, free-range eggs, unless stated otherwise.

• For recipes that require milk, you can use whole milk, low-fat, or skim.

Preheating the oven

Follow the temperature instructions within each recipe.

Special equipment

Keep an eye out for recipes that require special equipment. Buy or borrow items in advance.

Be allergy aware!
Always check that the ingredients for a recipe do not contain anything that you or a friend or anyone eating the cake may be allergic to or are not otherwise part of your recommended diet.

KITCHEN HYGIENE

Please note that when you're in the kitchen, you need to follow these important rules to keep germs in check.

• Always wash your hands before you start any recipe.

• Use hot, soapy water to clean cutting boards after each use.

• Keep your cooking area clean and have a cloth handy to wipe up any spills.

• Always check the use-by date on all ingredients.

• Wash your hands after handling raw eggs.

WEIGHTS AND MEASUREMENTS

Carefully measure the ingredients before you start a recipe. Use measuring spoons, weighing scales, and measuring cups, as necessary. Below are the abbreviations and full names for the measurements used in this book.

Metric	US measures	Spoon measures
g = gram	oz = ounce	tsp = teaspoon
kg = kilogram	lb = pound	tbsp = tablespoon
ml = milliliter	fl oz = fluid ounce	
cm = centimeter	in = inch	

Equipment

Here is the kitchen equipment that is used in this book. You won't need to use everything shown here for every recipe!

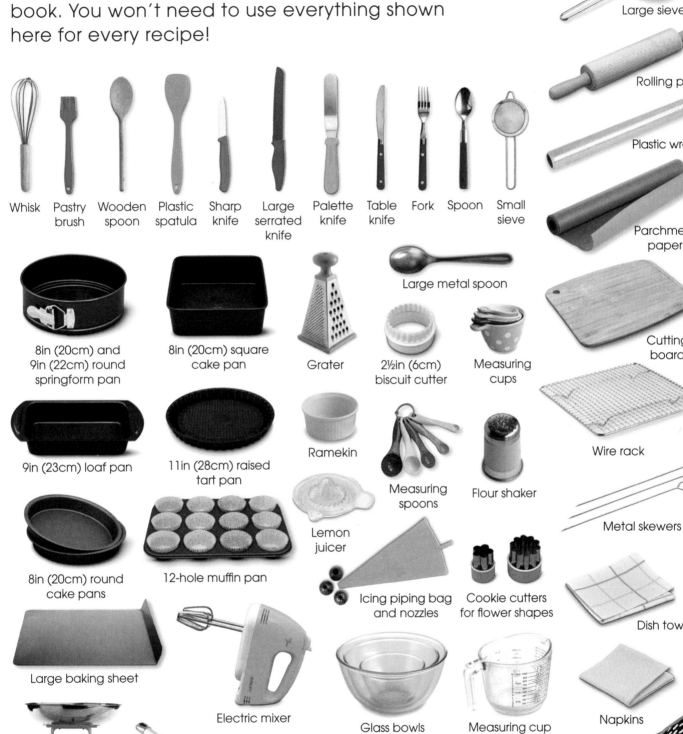

Large sieve

Rolling pin

Plastic wrap

Parchment paper

Whisk | Pastry brush | Wooden spoon | Plastic spatula | Sharp knife | Large serrated knife | Palette knife | Table knife | Fork | Spoon | Small sieve

Large metal spoon

8in (20cm) and 9in (22cm) round springform pan

8in (20cm) square cake pan

Grater

2½in (6cm) biscuit cutter

Measuring cups

Cutting board

9in (23cm) loaf pan

11in (28cm) raised tart pan

Ramekin

Measuring spoons

Flour shaker

Wire rack

Lemon juicer

Metal skewers

8in (20cm) round cake pans

12-hole muffin pan

Icing piping bag and nozzles

Cookie cutters for flower shapes

Dish towels

Large baking sheet

Electric mixer

Glass bowls

Measuring cup

Napkins

Weighing scales

Saucepan

Baking pans

9in (23cm) fluted tube pan

Oven mitts

Techniques for baking a cake

There are certain techniques in baking that you'll need to master. Once you know what's what, you'll be a baking expert. Refer to these pages when you're making the cakes in this book.

Grease a pan

1 Use some parchment paper to spread a thin layer of butter all over the bottom and sides of the pan.

Line a pan

1 Draw around your pan and add some extra for the parchment paper to go up the sides.

2 Position the parchment paper in the pan. Fold at the corners and snip off any extra pieces.

Sift

1 Shake flour or powdered sugar through a sieve to get rid of lumps and add air.

Fold

1 Use a spatula to mix gently, while keeping the air in the mixture.

2 Go around the edge of the bowl and then "cut" across, lifting as you go.

Separate an egg

1 Break the shell: tap the egg on the side of the bowl and open it up.

2 Transfer the yolk from half of one shell to the other, allowing the white to fall into the bowl.

Beat

1 Make a smooth, airy mixture by stirring fast with a wooden spoon.

Rub in

1 Rubbing in means to combine butter with flour until it looks like bread crumbs.

2 Using your fingertips, pick up the mixture, break up the lumps, and let it fall.

3 Keep rubbing your thumb along your fingertips until all the butter is mixed in.

Beat egg whites

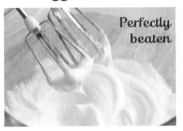

Perfectly beaten

1 Mix a lot of air into egg whites using an electric mixer, to create stiff peaks like these.

Overbeaten egg whites

2 The egg whites should be stiff; if you overbeat the mixture, it will collapse and look like this and you'll have to start again.

Cream

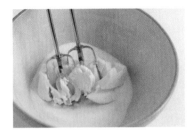

1 When mixing butter and sugar together, use butter that's been left to soften at room temperature.

2 Using an electric mixer or a wooden spoon, beat the butter and sugar together until pale in color, light, and fluffy.

Testing a cake is baked

1 A cake is baked when an inserted metal skewer comes out clean. .

Leveling a cake

1 If a cake isn't level, use a knife to carefully cut off the top of the cake.

Melting chocolate

1 Carefully melt chocolate pieces in a heatproof bowl over a pan of hot water. The bottom of the bowl should not touch the water.

2 Stir occasionally to distribute the heat. Heat until the chocolate is smooth and silky.

Victoria sponge cake

This classic treat is perfect for a party or as a special-occasion dessert, and it will be a hit with cake lovers! If you like, swap the jam for another fruity preserve.

40 mins prep | 20–25 mins baking, plus cooling | Serves 8–10

For the cake:
- 14 tbsp unsalted butter, softened, plus extra for greasing
- 1 cup sugar
- 4 eggs
- 1½ cups self-rising flour
- 1 tsp baking powder
- 1–2 tbsp milk
- mixed berries, to serve

For the filling:
- 7 tbsp unsalted butter, softened
- 1¼ cups powdered sugar, sifted
- ⅛ tsp vanilla extract
- 6 tbsp raspberry jam
- powdered sugar, for dusting

Special equipment:
- 2 x 8in (20cm) round cake pans

1 Preheat the oven to 350°F (180°C). Lightly grease the bottom and sides of the two cake pans and line the bottoms with parchment paper rounds.

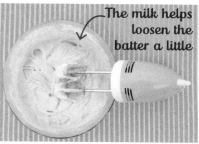

The milk helps loosen the batter a little

2 Put all the cake ingredients (except the milk) in a large bowl. Beat with an electric mixer until combined, then beat in the milk 1 tablespoon at a time, until the batter is smooth.

3 Divide the mixture equally between the two cake pans and smooth the surface with a spatula or the back of a spoon.

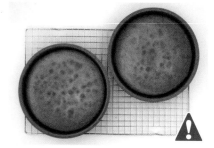

4 Bake side by side for 20–25 minutes, until golden brown. The cakes should have pulled away from the sides of the pans and be springy to the touch.

Cool bottom side up

5 Carefully place on a wire rack. Let cool in the pans for 5 minutes, then turn onto a wire rack and peel off the paper. Cool completely before filling.

Make the filling

6 Place the butter in a medium-sized bowl and beat with an electric mixer until smooth and creamy. Gradually beat in the powdered sugar and vanilla extract until smooth.

Serve with tasty, fresh berries.

If the butter and egg mixture starts to curdle, add 1 tbsp of flour.

7 Using a palette knife, spread the filling evenly over the flat side of one of the cakes, then gently spread the jam over the top. Top with the second sponge cake, flat sides together. Lightly dust with powdered sugar.

Lemon drizzle cake

This citrusy cake has a moist base and a delicious crunchy top, which is created by pouring the lemon glaze over the top of the cake while it's still warm.

20 mins prep | 35–40 mins baking, plus cooling | Makes 25 squares

For the cake:
- 14 tbsp unsalted butter, softened, plus extra for greasing
- finely grated zest and juice of 2 lemons, juice reserved for the syrup and icing (about 3 tbsp)
- 1 cup sugar
- 3 eggs, beaten
- 1½ cups self-rising flour
- 2 tbsp milk

For the syrup:
- ⅓ cup sugar

For the icing:
- ½ cup powdered sugar, sifted

Special equipment:
- 8in (20cm) square cake pan

Powdered sugar is regular sugar that's been crushed to a fine powder.

1 Preheat the oven to 350°F (180°C). Grease the bottom and sides of the pan and line the bottom with parchment paper.

2 Put the butter, lemon zest, and sugar in a mixing bowl and beat with an electric mixer until light and fluffy.

3 Beat in the eggs a little at a time. If the mixture starts to curdle, add 1 tablespoon of the flour. Fold in all the flour until you have a thick mixture, then stir in the milk until smooth.

4 Spoon the mixture into the pan and smooth the surface. Bake in the center rack of the oven for 35–40 minutes, until golden and pulling away from the sides of the pan.

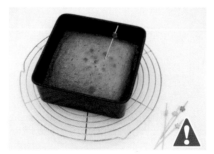

5 Carefully remove from the oven and place the pan on a wire rack. Prick the cake all over with a toothpick about 20 times.

6 To make the lemon syrup, place the sugar in a small mixing bowl and stir in 4 teaspoons of lemon juice until the sugar is dissolved. Drizzle the mixture slowly over the cake, so that it all sinks in.

The sweetness of the sugar offsets the tangy lemons.

7 Let cool in the pan for 15 minutes, then remove from the pan and place on the wire rack. Carefully remove the parchment paper.

8 Combine the powdered sugar in a bowl with the remaining lemon juice and stir until smooth. Drizzle the icing over the top of the cooled cake. When the icing has set, carefully cut the cake into 25 squares.

Light and fluffy

Classic cakes are often called sponge cakes because they are soft, springy, and full of small holes, just like a sponge. The holes are created by air bubbles, made when smart science works with the ingredients and mixing techniques, making cakes turn out tasty and light and fluffy.

Ingredients

A basic cake needs five main ingredients (others can be added to create different flavors and textures). Each ingredient has an important job to do and how much you use of each one is vital.

 Flour—When flour is mixed with water it makes a spongelike mixture. This makes cakes light and fluffy.

 Baking powder and baking soda—Both are rising (or leavening) agents. They make cakes rise. They do this by expanding air bubbles from a gas called carbon dioxide. Find out more on the next page.

 Sugar—During mixing, tiny air bubbles get trapped around the sugar crystals. They expand as the cake bakes, producing a light and airy texture. Sugar also helps hold on to water, which keeps a cake moist. Cakes without sugar are dense and not fluffy.

 Butter—Air bubbles form when butter and sugar are mixed together. This helps to make a cake light in texture.

 Eggs—Egg whites contain proteins which help to hold air during whisking and form a solid structure to a cake during baking.

Mixing

The way that different ingredients are mixed together affects a cake's texture. You want as much air in the cake batter as possible to make it light and fluffy. Here are some key mixing techniques.

 Beating—Mixing quickly and vigorously using a wooden spoon, electric mixer, or stand mixer. This combines the ingredients thoroughly and also adds air.

 Creaming—This specifically means beating sugar and (softened) butter together, by hand or with an electric mixer or stand mixer. Creaming adds air to the mixture, which changes the color, making it paler.

 Folding—This is a gentle way of mixing light ingredients (such as flour) with heavier ones (such as butter, sugar, and eggs). The lighter mixture is put on top of the heavier one and mixed with a gentle "down-across-up-and-over" folding action to keep as much air in the mixture as possible.

 Sifting—Also known as sieving, this means passing dry ingredients such as flour, cocoa powder, or powdered sugar through a sieve to remove lumps and make the ingredient lighter.

 Whisking—As the name suggests, this means mixing with a whisk (either a hand whisk or an electric mixer), which mixes quickly and adds air to the mixture. This is also sometimes called whipping.

A pinch of salt could also be considered a vital ingredient for a recipe. It can be added to enhance the cake's flavor.

Index

DK | Penguin Random House

Senior Editor Carrie Love
Project Art Editor Charlotte Bull
US Editor Margaret Parrish
US Senior Editor Shannon Beatty
Designed by Elaine Hewson
Production Editor Dragana Puvacic
Production Controller Francesca Sturiale
Jacket Designer Charlotte Bull
Jacket Editor Carrie Love
Illustrator Diego Vaisberg
Recipe writer Denise Smart
Additional editing Laura Nickoll and Catherine Saunders
Additional design Rachael Parfitt and Rachael Prokic
Managing Editor Penny Smith
Deputy Art Director Mabel Chan
Publishing Director Sarah Larter

First American Edition, 2022
Published in the United States by DK Publishing
1745 Broadway, 20th Floor, New York NY 10019

DK books are available at special discounts when purchased in bulk for
sales promotions, premiums, fund-raising, or educational use. For details,
contact: DK Publishing Special Markets, 1745 Broadway, 20th Floor, New
York NY 10019 SpecialSales@dk.com

Printed and bound in China

For the curious
www.dk.com

MIX
Paper | Supporting
responsible forestry
FSC™ C018179

This book was made with Forest
Stewardship Council™ certified
paper – one small step in DK's
commitment to a sustainable future.
For more information go to
www.dk.com/our-green-pledge

Acknowledgments

**Dorling Kindersley would like to thank the following people for
their assistance in the preparation of this book:** Caroline Stamps for
proofreading, Helen Peters for compiling the index, Denise Smart for being
the home economist at the shoots, Ruth Jenkinson for photography, Anne
Harnan for recipe testing, Clare Lloyd and Sif Nørskov for photo shoot
assistance, and Anne Damerell for legal assistance.

**Material used in this book was previously
published by DK in:**
The Children's Baking Book (2009),
Step-by-Step Baking (2011),
A Little Course in Baking (2013),
Step-by-Step Cake Decorating (2013),
Kids' Birthday Cakes Step by Step (2014),
Bake it (2019)

The publisher would like to thank the following for their kind permission to
reproduce their photographs:

(Key: a-above; b-below/bottom; c-center; f-far; l-left; r-right; t-top)

123RF.com: cloud7days 40cla, cokemomo 41crb, dionisvera 52bl,
g215 14bl, serezniy 38bl, Aninka Bongers-Sutherland 41bc, tobi 40tc, Olga
Yastremska 41cl; **Alamy Stock Photo:** JG Photography 12cla, Manivannan
Thirugnanasambandam 41tc; **Dorling Kindersley:** Ruth Jenkinson 1cb, 1b,
2, 2br, 3tr, 3cr, 3bl, 3br, 5tr, 5cla, 5cla (Brush), 5ca, 5ca (Knife), 5cra
(Board), 5cra (Knife), 5cra (Sieve), 5cl, 5cl (Flan), 5clb (Liners), 5clb (Tin),
5clb (Whisk), 5cb (Bag), 5cb (Juicer), 5crb, 5crb (Cutter), 5crb (Skewer), 5crb
(Towel), 5br, 5br (Glove), 10ca, 10cra, 10c, 10cr, 10cb, 10crb, 11, 11tc, 11tr,
12ca, 12cb, 14ca, 14cra, 14c, 14cr, 14cb, 14crb, 15, 20tr, 20cl, 20clb, 20clb
(Caramel), 20clb (Coconut), 20-21bc, 21cb, 21crb, 21br, 21br (Cola), 22ca,
22cra, 22c, 22cr, 22clb, 22cb, 22crb, 23, 23clb, 24c, 24-25b, 25tl, 25tc, 25tr,
25cla, 25ca, 25cra, 25clb, 25cb, 25crb, 28ca, 28cra, 28c, 28cr, 28cb, 28crb, 29,
29b, 30ca, 30cra, 30c, 30cr, 30cb, 30crb, 31, 31tc, 31tr, 31bl, 32ca, 32cra, 32c,
32cr, 32cb, 32crb, 32bl, 33clb, 33cb, 36b, 36-37, 37tc, 37tr, 37ca, 37cra, 37cb,
37crb, 38ca, 38cra, 38c, 38cr, 38cb, 38crb, 39, 39clb, 39cb, 39crb, 42ca, 42cra,
42c, 42cr, 42cb, 42crb, 43, 44ca, 44cra, 44c, 44cr, 44cb, 44crb, 45, 45clb,
45cb, 45crb, 46tl, 46ca, 46tr, 46bl, 46br, 47tl, 47tc, 47tr, 48ca, 48ca, 48cr,
48cb, 48br, 49cl, 49c, 49cr, 49clb, 49bc, 49br, 52ca, 52cra, 52c, 52cr, 52cb,
52crb, 53, 53clb, 56, 57tl, 57tc, 57tr, 57cla, 57ca, 57cra, 57b, 58ca, 58cra, 58c,
58cr, 58-59b, 59tl, 59tc, 59tr, 59cla, 59ca, 59cra, Mattel INC 5bl;
Dreamstime.com: Annapustynnikova 40crb, Bakerjim 24cb, Barbro Bergfeldt
20cla, Katerina Kovaleva 56bl, Svetlana Kuznetsova 12clb (Butter), Danelle
Mccollum 40clb, Serhii Milekhin 42clb, Roberts Resnais 21tl, Sommai
Sommai 42bl (Lemon), Vladimir Tomovic 8bl, Valentyn75 58bl

Cover images: Front: Dorling Kindersley: Ruth Jenkinson b, cb;
Back: Dorling Kindersley: Ruth Jenkinson clb, cb, crb

All other images © Dorling Kindersley

How do rising agents work?

Baking powder and baking soda both help cakes to rise. When added to water and heated, rising agents react with an acid (present in the rising agent itself or in the recipe, such as lemon juice) to produce carbon dioxide gas. This expands air bubbles occluded during mixing, with the formed carbon dioxide, helping the cake to rise and become light and fluffy.

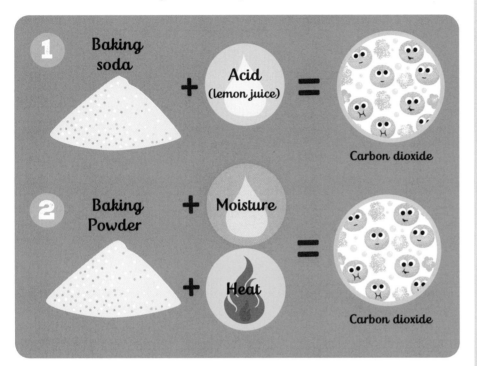

1. Baking soda + Acid (lemon juice) = Carbon dioxide
2. Baking Powder + Moisture + Heat = Carbon dioxide

Baking

Heat is another important part of making a light and fluffy cake. The oven must be at the right temperature and the cake must be baked for the right amount of time, so that air bubbles can expand and the cake can rise before its structure is set. Heat also helps create the texture, flavor, and aroma.

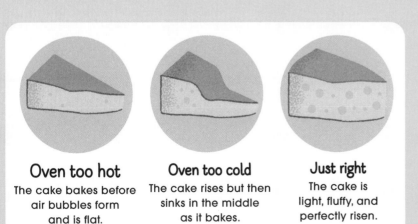

Oven too hot
The cake bakes before air bubbles form and is flat.

Oven too cold
The cake rises but then sinks in the middle as it bakes.

Just right
The cake is light, fluffy, and perfectly risen.

Question time

Q: Why is my cake dry?
A: This could be due to too much baking powder, the cake being overbaked or being left uncovered when cool.

Q: Why is my cake flat?
A: Did you use enough rising agent? Or perhaps the batter was overmixed and too much air was knocked out. The oven may have been too hot.

Q: How do I know if it's baked?
A: A well baked cake will feel springy when you touch it and shrink slightly from the sides of the pan. It should be a pale golden-brown color.

Q: Why did my cake sink?
A: The oven may have been too cold or the cake not fully baked.

Banana and pecan cake

It is best to use overripe bananas for this recipe, since they are extra sweet and help keep the cake moist and delicious. Nuts add nutrition and a crunchy texture to this dessert.

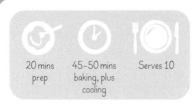

20 mins prep | 45–50 mins baking, plus cooling | Serves 10

For the cake:

- 7 tbsp unsalted butter, softened, plus extra for greasing
- 3 very ripe bananas, peeled
- 1 tsp lemon juice
- ¾ cup soft brown sugar
- 2 eggs, beaten
- 1 tsp vanilla extract
- 2¼ cups self-rising flour
- 1 tsp baking soda
- 1 tsp salt
- 1 tsp pumpkin pie spice
- ½ cup buttermilk
- ¾ cup pecans, toasted and chopped

For the frosting and decoration:

- 2 tbsp unsalted butter, softened
- 4½oz (125g) cream cheese
- 1 tsp vanilla extract
- 2–3 tbsp powdered sugar, sifted
- handful each of banana chips and chopped pecans

Special equipment:

- 9in (23cm) round springform pan

1 Preheat the oven to 350°F (180°C). Grease the bottom and sides of the pan. Line the bottom with parchment paper. Mash the bananas and lemon juice in a bowl until smooth.

3 Sift the flour and baking soda into the bowl with the banana mixture. Add the salt and pumpkin pie spice. Mix in the buttermilk. Stir in the nuts and pour into the pan.

Make the frosting

5 Put the butter in a bowl and beat with an electric mixer until smooth. Beat in the cream cheese, vanilla extract, and powdered sugar until combined.

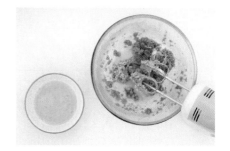

2 Put the butter and sugar in a bowl and beat with an electric mixer until light and fluffy. Beat in the eggs and vanilla extract a little at a time, then stir in the banana mixture.

Carefully remove the cake from the oven.

4 Bake for 45–55 minutes, until risen and a skewer inserted comes out clean. Cool in the pan on a wire rack for 20 minutes, then remove from the pan and peel off the parchment paper.

6 Using a palette knife, spread the frosting over the top of the cake, then decorate with banana chips and chopped pecans.

The cake will keep in an airtight container for up to 1 week.

All about eggs

Most cakes contain eggs. They help to bind all the other ingredients together. Most of the eggs we eat are laid by hens. Here's how eggs get from the farm to your local store.

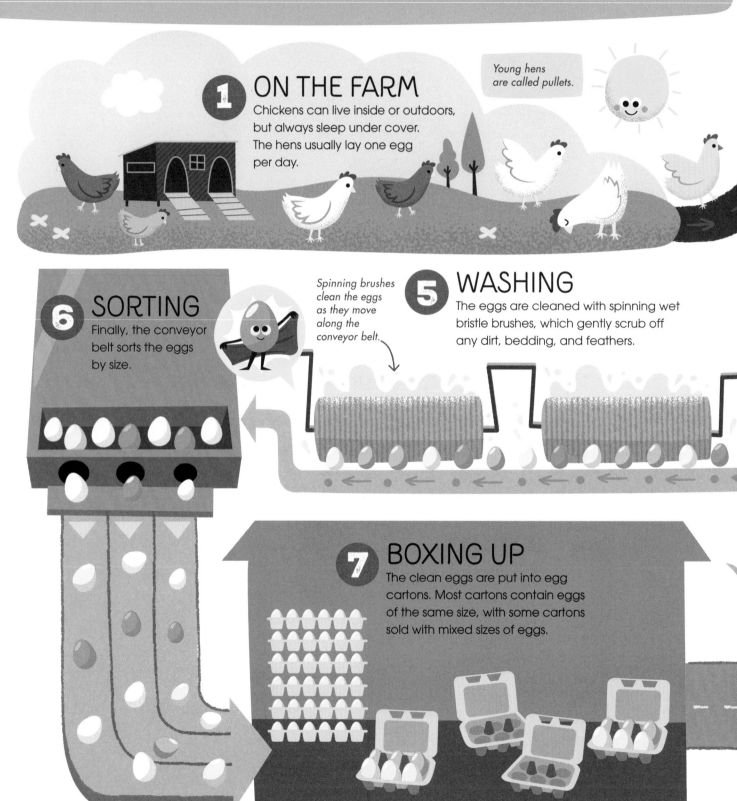

1 ON THE FARM
Chickens can live inside or outdoors, but always sleep under cover. The hens usually lay one egg per day.

Young hens are called pullets.

6 SORTING
Finally, the conveyor belt sorts the eggs by size.

Spinning brushes clean the eggs as they move along the conveyor belt.

5 WASHING
The eggs are cleaned with spinning wet bristle brushes, which gently scrub off any dirt, bedding, and feathers.

7 BOXING UP
The clean eggs are put into egg cartons. Most cartons contain eggs of the same size, with some cartons sold with mixed sizes of eggs.

2 HEALTHY HENS

Hens need to eat certain foods to keep them healthy. They are fed pellets, which contain everything they need.

Chicken-feed pellets

3 COLLECTING EGGS

Hens lay their eggs in nest boxes. The nest boxes are built on a tilt, so that the eggs can slowly roll out, sometimes onto a conveyor belt.

Hens like to lay their eggs in the same place every day.

4 CANDLING

A light is shone through the eggs to make sure they are not cracked and are safe to eat.

Candling lets us see what's inside an egg without actually opening it.

Good egg

Cracked egg

8 OFF THEY GO!

Finally, the eggs are sent off to supermarkets, bakeries, and factories. They are ready to be eaten or made into everything from cakes to mayonnaise.

SUPERMARKET

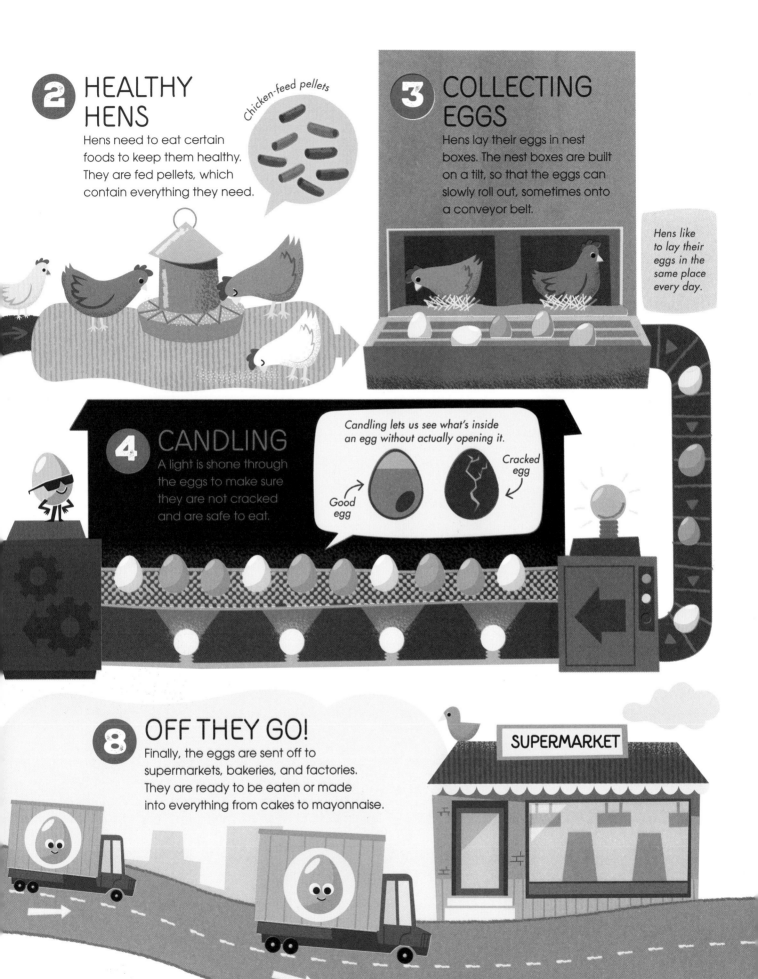

Yogurt cake

This traditional French baked treat is called "gâteau au yaourt." It's often the first cake that children in France are taught how to make. It's fluffy, light, and super tasty.

Serve on a large dish. →

10 mins prep

40–45 mins baking, plus cooling

Serves 8–10

For the cake:

- butter, for greasing
- ½ cup plain yogurt
- 1 cup light brown sugar
- 1 tsp vanilla extract
- ½ cup sunflower or vegetable oil
- 3 large eggs
- 1½ cups all-purpose flour
- 2 tsp baking powder
- ½ tsp salt
- powdered sugar, for dusting

Special equipment:

- 8in (20cm) round springform cake pan

Plain yogurt

When completely cool, dust with powdered sugar.

1 Preheat the oven to 350°F (180°C). Grease the bottom and sides of the pan and line the bottom with parchment paper.

2 Put the yogurt, sugar, vanilla extract, oil, and eggs in a large mixing bowl. Whisk with a fork or whisk until well blended.

3 Put the flour, baking powder, and salt in a mixing bowl and stir together.

4 Fold the flour mixture into the yogurt mixture and stir gently to combine, making sure there are no traces of flour.

5 Pour the batter into the prepared pan and bake in the oven for 40–45 minutes, until a skewer inserted into the center comes out clean. Cover the top with foil for the last 10 minutes if it's browning too quickly.

6 Carefully remove from the oven and cool in the pan on a wire rack for about 10 minutes, then remove from the pan (peeling off the paper) and cool completely on a wire rack.

When do you add the flavor?

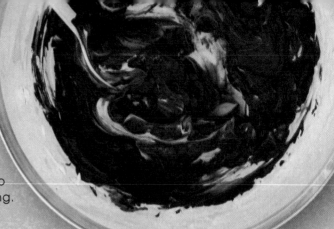

Powders, such as cocoa or dried ground spices, are usually added with the flour. Liquids and chunky ingredients are usually added to the cake batter during mixing.

Vanilla beans

Vanilla

Vanilla is a popular cake flavoring. It's most often used in liquid form, as a natural essence or extract, although it can also be found as a paste or as pod beans. Vanilla can be used on its own or to enhance other flavors, such as chocolate.

Detecting flavor

Your tongue has up to 10,000 taste buds, but some scientists think that up to 80 percent of your flavor perception is linked to smell.

Orange

Lemon

Coconut

Caramel

Cocoa versus chocolate

Cocoa or melted chocolate can be used to add chocolate flavor to cakes. Cocoa powder (see pages 48–49) can replace a little of the flour and gives an intense flavor. Melted chocolate can be mixed in with the butter and gives a sweeter, softer flavor and a "fudgier" texture. You can also use a mixture of both, or simply fold in chocolate chips before baking.

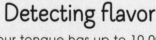
Cocoa powder

Chocolate bar

Extracts

In addition to vanilla, other extracts, such as peppermint or almond, can be added. In fact, most flavors can be found as an extract, and they're really easy to add to cakes. The taste can be very strong, however, so you only need to use a little bit.

Mixed fruit

Fruits and nuts

Dried fruits and chopped nuts add flavor and texture to a cake and are usually mixed in just before baking. Fruitcake is a special type of cake that contains lots of dried fruits. It has a heavier texture and richer taste than sponge cakes.

CAN YOU CHANGE THE FLAVOR IN A RECIPE?

Most flavors are easy to swap out if you don't like the one in the recipe. You can substitue chocolate chips for raisins, ground ginger for cinnamon, peppermint extract for vanilla extract. You just need to add the same amount that's stated in the recipe.

Almonds

Flavor

Most cakes have five basic ingredients (see pages 12-13), but flavors can be added in the form of powders, liquids, or chunky ingredients that affect the texture, too.

Star anise

Lemon

Cinnamon

Pineapple

Ginger

Raspberry powder

Banana added to a cake mixture

Fresh fruit

Fresh or canned fruits add great flavor to cakes, but they can make the batter very wet. Mashed bananas are the easiest fruit to bake with, since they can be mixed into the batter. Other fruits, such as berries, can sink to the bottom of the batter when baking. You can cut them up into small pieces and mix them into the batter to prevent this.

Carrot cake

Unusual flavors

Some really unusual flavors can work surprisingly well in cakes. Rose water, cola, miso, and tea combine well with traditional sweet ingredients.

Vegetables

Vegetables may seem like an unusual choice, but carrots, sweet potatoes, zucchini, beets, and pumpkins all work really well. They add fiber to the cake, which is good for your health.

Matcha tea powder

Cola

Marble cake

Chocolate and vanilla cake mixtures are swirled together to make this marbled cake. It is delicious cold or served hot with custard or whipped cream as a dessert.

15 mins prep	30 mins baking, plus cooling	Makes 25 squares

For the cake:

- 12 tbsp unsalted butter, softened, plus extra for greasing
- 1 cup sugar
- 3 large eggs, beaten
- 2 tsp vanilla extract
- 1⅓ cups self-rising flour
- 2 tbsp cocoa powder

Special equipment:

- 8in (20cm) square cake pan

1 Preheat the oven to 350°F (180°C). Grease the bottom and sides of the pan and line the bottom with parchment paper.

2 Put the butter and sugar in a large bowl and beat with an electric mixer until light and fluffy, then mix in the eggs, a little at a time, beating well after each addition. Beat in the vanilla extract.

3 Gently fold in the flour, until the mixture is well combined and smooth.

4 Spoon half of the mixture into the pan, leaving spaces between the dollops.

5 Sift the cocoa powder over the remaining mixture in the bowl and stir until combined. Spoon the chocolate mixture between the plain dollops.

6 Gently smooth the top, leveling the cake and filling in any holes. Then, using a table knife, drag the mixture together to create a swirl effect.

For a twist, add 1 teaspoon of orange flavoring to the cake mixture.

Perfectly golden

⚠️

7 Bake in the center rack of the oven for 30 minutes, until well risen and springy to the touch. Let cool in the pan for 10 minutes, then turn onto a wire cooling rack and remove the parchment paper. Allow to cool completely, then carefully cut into 25 squares.

Carrot cake

This cake will be a great favorite with carrot lovers! The oil and syrup make the cake extra moist, and the cream cheese frosting adds a bit of sweetness to every bite.

30 mins prep	25–30 mins baking, plus cooling	Serves 10–12

For the cake:
- butter, for greasing
- 1 cup sunflower or vegetable oil
- ⅓ cup buttermilk or plain yogurt
- 4 large eggs
- 1½ tsp vanilla extract
- 2¼ cups self-rising flour
- 1½ cups light brown sugar
- 2 tsp ground cinnamon
- ½ tsp ground ginger
- ¼ nutmeg, finely grated
- 1 cup grated carrots (about 3)
- ¾ cup golden raisins or raisins
- 1 tbsp freshly grated orange zest
- ¾ cup coarsely chopped walnuts or pecans (or a mixture of both)

For the frosting:
- 4 tbsp unsalted butter, softened
- 9oz (250g) cream cheese
- 3 tsp finely grated orange zest
- 3 tsp orange juice
- ½ cup powdered sugar, sifted

For decoration:
- 12 walnut halves
- 2 tsp grated orange zest

Special equipment:
- 2 x 8in (20cm) round cake pans

Space the walnuts evenly.

To save time, grate the carrots in a food processor.

1 Preheat the oven to 350°F (180°C). Lightly grease the bottoms and sides of the two round cake pans and line them with parchment paper rounds. ⚠

2 In a measuring cup, whisk together the oil, buttermilk or yogurt, eggs, and vanilla extract.

3 Put the flour, sugar, spices, grated carrots, golden raisins or raisins, orange zest, and nuts in a large bowl and mix well. Pour in the wet ingredients from the cup and stir well to mix.

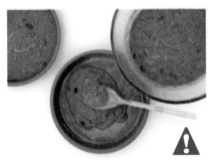

4 Pour the mixture evenly into the pans. Bake in the oven side by side for 25–30 minutes, until springy to the touch. A skewer inserted into the center should come out clean. ⚠

5 Carefully remove from the oven and place on a wire rack. Leave to cool in the pans for 10 minutes, then turn onto the rack and peel off the parchment paper. Let cool completely. ⚠

Make the frosting

6 Put the butter in a bowl and beat with an electric mixer until smooth, then beat in the cream cheese, orange zest and juice, and powdered sugar. Beat until well mixed.

Carrots give this cake an amazing texture.

7 Spread half the frosting over the flat side of one of the cakes. Lay the other cake on top, flat-side down, and spread the remaining frosting over it.

8 Arrange 11 of the walnut halves around the edge of the cake and 1 in the middle, then scatter the orange zest on top.

Flour

Most cakes contain flour. Flour is made by milling grains, such as wheat. When mixed with water and fat, such as butter, flour is what gives cakes and bread their structure and texture. Here's how a little grain is turned into a baking superstar.

Humans have been making flour for 6,000 years. Before machinery, they used stones to crush wheat.

1 GROWING

Wheat grows in large fields. It is then cut by a combine harvester, which separates the grains and the stalks.

The grain is taken to a mill to be turned into flour.

Each grain of wheat is a seed that would grow more wheat if planted.

2 CLEANING AND GRISTING

Wheat is turned into flour at a mill. First, the grain must be cleaned to remove the chaff (the outside of the grain) and any stones or leaves.

Any stalks or mud are also removed in this machine.

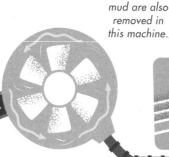

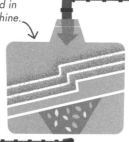

The process of separating wheat grains from their chaff is called gristing.

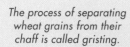

Larger rollers split the grain.

3 MILLING

Water is added to the grains, which are then separated by rollers into three parts: the bran layer (outer skin), the endosperm (food store), and the germ (the part that makes a new grain if planted). The bran layer is kept to make whole-wheat flour. White flour is made from ground-up endosperm and germ.

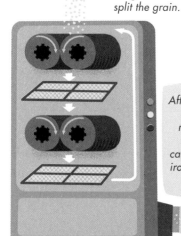

After rolling, extra nutrients such as calcium and iron may be added.

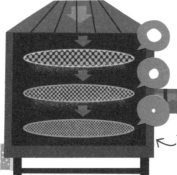

This machine is called a plansifter.

4 BAGGING

The flour is quality checked and put in big sacks. If it's going to the supermarket, it will be packed in smaller bags.

Baking powder

At this stage, a rising agent, such as baking powder, may be added to make self-rising flour.

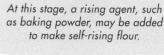

Butter

Butter, or some other kind of fat or oil, is essential in a cake to add flavor. It also works with the flour and sugar to create a light, fluffy texture. Butter is a dairy product, and it can be used cold, at room temperature, or melted. But how is it made?

1 MILKING

Butter starts with milk. Today, dairy cows are milked by machines instead of by hand. The milk is taken away via pipes and stored in large, cool vats.

2 TRANSPORTING

A tanker takes the milk from the farm to a dairy or factory. Here, it can become different types of milk or milk products, such as cheese or yogurt, as well as butter.

To make butter, the milk has to be separated into two parts, the fat and the liquid.

3 PROCESSING

The milk is poured into a centrifuge machine to separate the fat (cream) from the liquid (buttermilk). The cream is then pasteurized (heated to kill any bacteria). It's then cooled before being churned, which is when the butter granules separate from the buttermilk.

After heating, another machine churns the milk.

Before it is separated, the milk must be heated.

4 CHURNING

The butter granules may be washed with water to remove any buttermilk. The butter is churned again and squeezed through perforated plates to remove any remaining liquid.

Salt may be added at this stage, but a lot of butter is unsalted.

5 COOLING AND SHAPING

The butter is then cooled and shaped into large blocks. The blocks are cut into smaller blocks and packaged, ready to be transported to stores and supermarkets.

German apple cake

This cake is popular in Germany and is called "apfelkuchen." Make it the day before you plan to eat it, as this gives the apples more time to infuse the cake with their flavor.

15 mins prep	45–50 mins baking, plus cooling	Serves 8–10

For the cake:

- 8 tbsp unsalted butter, softened, plus extra for greasing
- 3 sweet-tart apples, such as Honey Crisp or Jonagold, cored, peeled, and cut into thin wedges
- 1 tbsp lemon juice
- ¾ cup light brown sugar
- 3 eggs, beaten
- 1½ cups all-purpose flour
- 2 tsp baking powder
- ½ tsp salt
- 4 tbsp milk
- whipped cream, to serve

For the topping:

- ½ tsp ground cinnamon
- 1 tbsp demerara sugar

Special equipment:

- 8in (20cm) round springform pan

1 Preheat the oven to 325°F (170°C). Grease the bottom and sides of the pan and line the bottom with parchment paper. Put the apple wedges in a bowl and coat with the lemon juice.

2 Put the butter and sugar in a large bowl and beat with an electric mixer until light and fluffy. Beat in the eggs, a little at a time, until smooth.

3 Combine the flour, baking powder, and salt in a bowl. Gently fold the mixture into the wet mixture. Slowly add the milk, mixing well after each addition, until smooth.

4 Spoon the mixture into the pan and smooth the surface. Arrange the apple wedges, flat-side down, in a spiral pattern, starting at the outside edge and working to the center.

5 Mix the cinnamon and sugar in a small bowl, then sprinkle it over the apples. Bake in the center rack of the oven for 45–50 minutes, until golden, or until a skewer comes out clean.

6 Carefully place the pan on a wire rack. Let cool in the pan for 10 minutes. Remove from the pan and peel off the paper. Let cool on the rack.

If necessary, cover the top with foil in the oven to prevent the cake from burning.

It's delicious served warm with whipped cream.

New York cheesecake

This popular style of cheesecake originated in the the United States during the 1870s. New York-style cheesecake is so creamy and delicious because of the sour cream.

15 mins prep | 45–55 mins baking, plus 3 hrs chilling | Serves 8

For the base:
- 4 tbsp unsalted butter, softened, plus extra for greasing
- 7oz (200g) graham crackers (about 1½ cups crumbs)
- 1 tbsp sugar

For the filling:
- 21oz (600g) cream cheese
- 1 cup sugar
- 1 cup sour cream
- 3 large eggs
- 1 tsp vanilla extract
- finely grated zest of 1 lemon
- ½ cup all-purpose flour, sifted

For the sour cream topping:
- ½ cup sour cream
- 2 tsp sugar
- 2 tsp lemon juice
- blueberries, to serve

Special equipment:
- 8in (20cm) round springform cake pan

Lemons and sour cream

1 Preheat the oven to 325°F (160°C) and lightly grease the bottom and sides of the pan.

2 To make the base, crush the crackers in a food processor to fine crumbs. Alternatively, crush them in a sealed plastic food bag wrapped in a dish towel.

3 Melt the butter in a large saucepan. Stir in the crackers and sugar, then press the mixture into the bottom of the pan with the back of a spoon. Chill for 15 minutes.

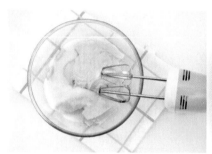

4 Put the cream cheese, sugar, and sour cream in a medium-sized bowl and beat with an electric mixer until smooth.

5 Gently beat in the eggs, one at a time, then add the vanilla extract and lemon zest. Using a spoon, fold in the flour to form a smooth batter.

6 Pour the filling over the base. Place the pan on a baking sheet and bake for 45–55 minutes, until the top is golden and the cheesecake is set at the edges but still wobbly in the middle.

The cream is nearly as sour as a lemon!

7 Carefully remove from the oven. Cool completely in the pan on a rack. Put in the fridge to set for 3 hours, or overnight.

8 Carefully remove the collar from the cake pan. To make the topping, place the sour cream, sugar, and lemon juice in a small bowl and mix well, then spoon over the top of the cake in a thin, even layer.

The cream is sour because it has been fermented.

Chocolate cake

This cake is perfect for celebrating a birthday or as a special treat! The sunflower oil makes the cake moist and helps it stay fresh longer, and the frosting is superrich and luxurious.

35 mins prep, plus chilling | 25–30 mins baking, plus cooling | Serves 12

For the cake:

- butter, for greasing
- 1¼ cups self-rising flour
- ¼ cup cocoa powder
- 1 tsp baking powder
- ½ tsp baking soda
- ¾ cup light brown sugar
- ⅔ cup sunflower or vegetable oil
- 3 eggs, beaten
- ½ cup sour cream
- 1 tbsp honey
- 1 tbsp corn syrup
- raspberries, to serve

For the frosting:

- 3½oz (100g) dark chocolate (minimum 70%), broken into small pieces
- 8 tbsp unsalted butter, softened
- 1 cup powdered sugar
- 1 tsp vanilla extract

Special equipment:

- 2 x 8in (20cm) round cake pans

Cocoa powder

1 Preheat the oven to 350°F (180°C). Lightly grease the bottom and sides of the two pans and line the bottoms with parchment paper rounds.

2 Sift the flour, cocoa powder, baking powder, and baking soda into a large bowl. Add the light brown sugar and mix well.

3 Make a well in the center, add the oil, eggs, sour cream, honey, and syrup. Beat well with an electric mixer until smooth.

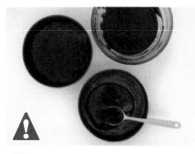

4 Divide the mixture evenly between the pans and bake side by side on the center rack of the oven for 25–30 minutes, until risen. The cakes should be springy to the touch.

5 Carefully remove from the oven and place on a wire rack. Leave to cool in the pans for 5 minutes, then turn onto the rack and peel off the paper.

Now, make the frosting

6 Melt the chocolate in a heatproof bowl set over a pan of simmering water or in the microwave on medium power for 2–3 minutes (stirring every 20–30 seconds). Let it cool slightly.

This cake is a real crowd-pleaser!

Chocolate cake goes well with raspberries.

7 Beat the butter in a large bowl with an electric mixer until soft. Sift in the powdered sugar and beat again until combined and light and fluffy. Beat in the vanilla extract.

8 Add the chocolate and stir until smooth and creamy. Spread the frosting on the flat side of one cake using a palette knife. Top with the second cake, flat-side down.

All about sugar

Sugar makes cakes taste sweet. It also helps to create a light and airy cake by trapping air bubbles around its edges that expand as the cake bakes. Let's find out about the two main types of sugar.

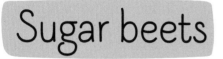

Sugar beets

1 GROWING

Sugar beets are root vegetables grown in cooler, temperate climates. They are harvested by a big machine that pulls the roots from the soil and chops off the leaves.

The leafy tops of the plants can be used for animal feed.

The sugar is stored in the thick root.

The roots still have lots of mud on them when they're picked.

People only thought of extracting sugar from beets in the late 18th century. The vegetable is grown in cooler places, such as Europe and the US.

2 OFF TO THE FACTORY

The sugar beets are taken to the factory and then washed. Next, they are sliced into thin strips called cossettes.

Beets are sliced

Beets are washed

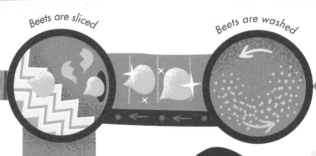
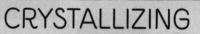

The sugar can then be bagged and sent off to be sold.

Sugar crystals

Hot water is added

3 PURIFYING

Hot water is added to the cossettes to extract the sugar. A lime solution (made from limestone) is added to the raw juice to remove any impurities. It is now a syrup. Any remaining cossettes are fed into screw presses, which extract the remaining juice.

4 CRYSTALLIZING

The syrup is filtered further and then heated. Tiny sugar crystals are added to start the crystallization process. The syrup transforms into sugar crystals. Any impurities in the syrup are separated in a centrifugal sugar machine. The sugar crystals are washed, dried, and cooled.

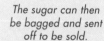

Sugar

Cane sugar

1 HARVESTING

Sugar cane grows best in warm, tropical places with plenty of sunshine and rain. A big machine cuts the sugar-cane stalks and then feeds them into a container on a second vehicle.

The sugar is stored in the stalks.

The harvester leaves the bottom of the stalks so that they can grow again.

2 AT THE MILL

The cut cane is taken to a mill and washed thoroughly. The stalks are then cut or shredded and crushed.

About 80 percent of the world's sugar comes from sugar cane.

3 SEPARATING AND EVAPORATING

The mixture travels to the separator machine, which separates it into juice and pulp. The juice then heads to the evaporator, where it is heated to remove any last bits of pulp and to reduce it to a thick syrup.

The stalks are crushed here

Syrup

Juice

Pulp

Pulp

The sugar-cane pulp is used to make fuel and animal feed.

Sugar crystals

4 CRYSTALLIZATION

When the syrup is cool, a small amount of sugar is added, to start the crystallization process. The mixture is then spun to remove any remaining liquid. The result is sugar crystals.

5 PURIFICATION

The sugar heads to a granulator machine to be purified and dried. It is then passed through mesh to remove any remaining impurities and give the sugar its required consistency.

Now, the sugar can be put into sacks or bags and sent to factories, stores, supermarkets, and restaurants.

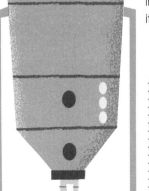

Sugar

Sugar

Honey cake

Honey is a fantastic alternative to sugar for sweetening cakes. When baking this rich cake, make sure to use a honey with a good floral flavor, such as orange blossom honey.

| 15 mins prep | 45–50 mins baking, plus cooling | Serves 8–10 |

For the cake:
- 8 tbsp unsalted butter, melted and cooled, plus extra for greasing
- 1½ cups honey
- 3 eggs
- ½ cup sour cream or Greek yogurt
- 1 tsp vanilla extract
- 2 cups all-purpose flour
- 2 tsp baking powder
- ½ tsp baking soda
- ½ tsp salt

For the glaze:
- 2 tbsp butter
- 2 tbsp honey

Special equipment:
- 8in (20cm) round springform cake pan

Use clear honey for this recipe.

Allow the glaze to set, then serve the cake in slices.

My honey helped make this!

1 Preheat the oven to 350°F (180°C). Grease the bottom and sides of the pan and line the bottom with parchment paper.

2 Put the melted butter, honey, eggs, sour cream or yogurt, and vanilla extract in a large bowl and whisk together until smooth.

3 Combine the flour, baking powder, baking soda, and salt in a bowl and mix together. Gently fold the flour mixture into the wet mixture until just combined.

4 Pour the batter into the pan and bake in the oven for 45–50 minutes, or until a skewer inserted into the center of the cake comes out clean. If the top starts to get too dark, cover with foil for the last 5 minutes.

5 Carefully remove from the oven and place on a wire rack. Allow to cool in the pan for 15 minutes, then turn onto the rack and peel off the parchment paper. Let cool completely.

6 To make the honey glaze, put the butter and honey in a small pan and melt together, stirring occasionally. Let cool for a few minutes, until thickened slightly, then spoon over the cake.

Strawberry shortcakes

The crumbly texture of these tasty, biscuit-like shortcakes goes perfectly with the smooth cream and fruity strawberry filling. They're easy to make and will impress your friends and family.

20 mins prep   12–15 mins baking, plus cooling   Makes 6

For the shortcakes:
- 5 tbsp cold, unsalted butter, diced into ½in (1cm) cubes, plus extra for greasing
- 2 cups all-purpose flour, plus extra for dusting
- ¼ cup sugar, plus extra for dusting
- 1 tbsp baking powder
- ¼ tsp salt
- ⅓ cup milk
- ⅓ cup heavy cream, plus a little extra to glaze

For the compote:
- 10oz (300g) strawberries, hulled and halved (or quartered if large)
- 1 tbsp sugar

For the filling:
- 10oz (300g) strawberries, hulled and sliced
- 2 tbsp sugar
- 1¼ cups heavy cream
- 1 tsp vanilla extract

Special equipment:
- large baking sheet
- 2½in (6cm) biscuit cutter

1 Preheat the oven to 400°F (200°C). Grease the baking sheet.

2 Put the flour, sugar, baking powder, and salt in a large bowl and mix together. Add the cubes of butter and, using your fingertips, rub together to form coarse crumbs.

3 Stir in the milk and cream until the crumbs start to come together. The dough should still be slightly wet. Stir well to mix.

4 Place the mixture onto a lightly floured surface and press together to form a dough. Pat out a round ¾in (2cm) thick.

5 Cut out 6 rounds with the biscuit cutter, place on the baking sheet, brush with a little extra cream, and sprinkle with sugar. Bake for 12–15 minutes, until golden. Cool on a wire rack.

6 Make the strawberry compote by placing the strawberries in a pan with the sugar. Simmer for about 5 minutes until collapsed. Leave to cool.

Use spare dough to make more!

7 For the filling, place the sliced strawberries in a bowl and stir in 1 tablespoon of the sugar. Set aside to macerate (soften).

8 Put the cream, remaining tablespoon of sugar, and the vanilla extract in a bowl and whip with an electric mixer until the mixture forms soft peaks.

9 Using a serrated knife, carefully cut the cakes in half. Layer the bottom halves with the strawberries and cream, then drizzle the compote over the top. Add the lids and serve.

Mochi

This traditional Japanese rice cake is often eaten on New Year's Eve.

Boterkoek

Boterkoek (butter cake) is a simple Dutch cake made with butter, flour, sugar, eggs, and almond extract. It is often served with a hot drink as a tasty snack.

Types of cake

Every culture in the world has special cakes. Some might be everyday favorites, while others are more elaborate, baked to celebrate special events. Take a look at some delicious creations from around the world.

Sachertorte

This Austrian specialty is a rich chocolate cake, containing butter, sugar, eggs, chocolate, flour, and apricot jam.

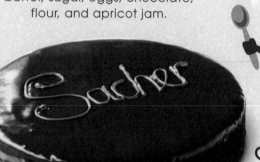

Schwarzwälder Kirschtorte

Chocolate, cherries, and cream flavor this popular German cake, which translates as Black Forest cherry cake.

Tres—leche cake

Tres leches means "three milks," but this Mexican layer cake actually contains four milky components: whole milk, condensed milk, evaporated milk, and cream.

Panettone

This Italian Christmas favorite is technically a sweet bread, not a cake, since it contains yeast.

South Indian honey cake

This light cake is a traditional southern Indian baked good. It does not contain eggs and is covered with a sticky honey or jam glaze and sometimes dried, shredded coconut, too.

Madeleines

These small buttery French treats are baked in a special mold to give them their distinctive scallop shape.

Paskha

This Russian cheesecake is served at Easter and has two special features— its pyramid shape and the fact that it's chilled, not baked.

Lamington

This traditional Australian vanilla sponge cake is cut into squares and coated with chocolate frosting and shredded coconut.

Malva pudding

This sweet, sticky South African cake has apricot jam in the batter and in the syrupy sauce that covers it.

Sponge styles

There are lots of varieties and flavors of cake, but most are based around a few general styles of sponge cake.

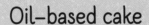

Butter cake

This basic sponge cake involves creaming butter and sugar together before adding eggs and dry ingredients. Many flavors can be added.

Oil-based cake

This sponge cake contains oil, not butter, to give it a moist texture. It is often baked with baking soda and baking powder. Carrot cake is a popular example.

Loaf cake

This simple cake, also known as pound cake, has equal amounts of butter, sugar, and flour. It is baked in a loaf pan and is sometimes called "bread."

Chiffon cake

This cake contains baking powder and vegetable oil. Egg whites are beaten to soft peaks, then folded into the batter to create a light sponge cake with a soft crumb and a rich flavor.

No rising agent

Instead of rising agents, air is added by whipping the eggs. This type of sponge cake is often called a "genoise" and is great for layered or rolled-up cakes.

Flourless cake

You can add air to a flourless cake by beating the egg whites to soft peaks. You can also use ground almonds or polenta instead of flour.

Lime and coconut cake

This cake is baked in a fluted tube pan with a hole in the middle. Tube pans come in lots of sizes and patterns and are perfect for holiday and celebration cakes. The coconut and lime add great texture to this cake.

30 mins prep

35–40 mins baking, plus cooling

Serves 10–12

For the cake:

- 16 tbsp unsalted butter, softened, plus extra for greasing
- 2¼ cups sugar
- finely grated zest and juice of 4 limes (about ¼ cup)
- 4 large eggs, beaten
- 1 cup unsweetened, shredded coconut
- 2 cups self-rising flour

For the icing:

- finely grated zest and juice of 1 lime (2–3 tbsp)
- 1 cup powdered sugar
- 2 tbsp unsweetened, shredded coconut, toasted in a pan over medium heat for 2 minutes (stirring continuously)

Special equipment:

- 9in (23cm) fluted tube pan

↖ Lime and coconut

1 Preheat the oven to 350°F (180°C). Generously butter the inside of the pan, using a pastry brush to get right into the corners of the pan.

2 Put the butter, sugar, and lime zest in a large mixing bowl and beat with an electric mixer until light and fluffy. Beat in the eggs a little at a time, beating well after each addition.

3 Fold in the coconut and flour, then stir in the lime juice. Spoon into the pan and smooth the top. Bake for 35–40 minutes, until risen and golden.

4 Remove from the oven and place on a wire rack. Leave to cool in the pan for 10 minutes, then turn onto the rack and let cool completely.

Now, make the icing

5 Put the lime juice in a bowl and sift the powdered sugar over the top. Stir until smooth. It should easily run off a spoon. Stir in half the lime zest.

6 Place the cake on a plate. Drizzle the icing over the cake, then sprinkle with the remaining lime zest and the coconut.

Let the icing drizzle down to the plate.

Serve up slices for dessert.

43

Celebration cake

Ideal for a birthday party, this light and fluffy, multilayered sponge cake is flavored with vanilla, strawberry, and pistachio. Coated in a strawberry frosting, it is finished with a pretty chocolate drip.

2 hrs, plus 1 hr chilling

25–30 mins, plus cooling

Serves 12–14

For the cake:

- 15 tbsp unsalted butter, softened, plus extra for greasing
- 1¾ cups sugar
- 2 tsp vanilla extract
- 6 eggs
- 2¾ cups self-rising flour
- 1 tsp baking soda
- ½ cup ground pistachio nuts
- green, pink, and violet gel food coloring
- 7–8 fresh strawberries, hulled and halved, to decorate
- purple fondant icing, for shapes, to decorate, plus powdered sugar for rolling, to decorate

For the frosting:

- 12 tbsp unsalted butter, softened
- 5 cups powdered sugar, sifted
- 2–3 tbsp strawberry sauce

For the chocolate drip:

- 2½oz (75g) dark chocolate (70–75%), finely chopped
- ⅔ cup heavy cream

Special equipment:

- 3 x 8in (20cm) round cake pans
- piping bag and star-shaped nozzle
- small star-shaped cutter

1 Preheat the oven to 350°F (180°C). Grease the bottom and sides of the pans and line with parchment paper. Make the strawberry sauce.

2 Put the butter and sugar in a large bowl and beat with an electric mixer until light and fluffy, then beat in the vanilla extract.

3 Add the eggs, one at a time, beating well. Fold in the flour and baking soda. Divide the mixture equally into 4 bowls. Set aside 1 bowl.

4 Fold the pistachios and 1 tsp green food coloring into 1 bowl. Fold 3 tbsp of strawberry sauce and 1 tsp pink food coloring into 1 bowl. Fold 1 tsp violet food coloring into 1 bowl.

5 Put dollops of each mixture into the pans. Gently smooth the top of each cake mixture.

6 Bake for 25–30 minutes, until golden and springy to the touch. Carefully remove from the oven and turn onto wire racks. Peel off the parchment paper.

44

For the strawberry sauce:

- 7oz (200g) fresh strawberries, hulled and halved
- 1 tbsp sugar

To make the strawberry sauce, puree the strawberries in a blender, pour into a small pan, and add the sugar. Simmer gently for 10 minutes, until reduced by half, then let cool.

The strawberry sauce gives the frosting a fruity flavor.

7 To make the frosting, beat the butter with half the powdered sugar in a bowl using a handheld or stand mixer. Beat in the rest of the powdered sugar until light and fluffy.

8 Mix 2–3 tablespoons of the strawberry sauce and a few drops of pink food coloring into the frosting.

9 When the cakes are cool, carefully level the tops, if necessary, using a serrated knife, to prepare them for frosting. Turn to page 46 for further instructions.

Celebration cake—the final touches (see pages 44–45)

First, crumb-coat the cake

1 Spread the sides and top of the cake with a thin layer of frosting to cover the entire cake, filling any gaps between the sponge cakes. Chill the cake in the fridge for 30 minutes.

Next, frost the cake

2 Pile the frosting on top (reserve a little), then use a palette knife to ease it over the edge and down the sides. Make it as smooth as you can. Chill for 30 minutes.

Now, make the chocolate drip

3 Put the chocolate in a bowl. Place the cream in a small pan and heat gently, until just steaming. Pour onto the chocolate, leave for 30 seconds, then stir gently, until glossy. Let cool.

Frosting cakes

Frosting is a fantastic way to decorate your cakes! Here's how to frost a special occasion cake and pipe frosting onto cupcakes. The more you practice, the neater your frosting will be.

Filling a piping bag

1 Fit the nozzle onto the piping bag and place the bag upright in a tall glass. Open out the bag, folding back the sides over the rim of the glass and spoon in the frosting.

2 Squeeze the frosting toward the nozzle, then lay the bag down. Twist the bag at the top to seal it. Squeeze the top of the bag (below the twist) to get the frosting to come out.

Frosting cupcakes—the final touches (see pages 48–49)

1 To frost the top of the cupcake, hold the nozzle ½in (1cm) straight above the cupcake and pipe from the outside edge inward in a spiral. Apply pressure so that an even amount comes out.

2 Build several layers of frosting in a spiral movement, making each layer slightly smaller as you go. Release the pressure to end the spiral at the center of the cupcake.

4 Spoon the chocolate drip over the top edge of the cake. Fill in the middle of the top of the cake with the chocolate drip.

5 Place the remaining frosting in a piping bag tipped with a star nozzle. Pipe a ring around the top edge of the cake. Place half a fresh strawberry in each dollop of frosting.

6 Lightly dust the worktop with powdered sugar and roll out the purple fondant. Using your shaped cutter, cut out the shapes. Stick them around the bottom of the cake.

How to frost a cake

Crumb-coat the cake

Now, frost the cake

1 Place a dollop of frosting on the top and swirl the frosting over the whole surface as you spin the cake on a lazy Susan. Chill for 30 minutes.

2 With the cake on the lazy Susan, put a dollop of buttercream frosting onto the center of the top of the cake.

3 Using a palette knife, swirl and smooth the frosting, spreading it outward and over the sides as you go.

4 Turn the cake as you spread the frosting down and around the sides, to cover it evenly. When smooth, let the cake set for 10 minutes, then repeat.

5 Put the knife blade in a cup of boiling water. Dry it and run it around the sides of the cake, turning the cake around with the flat surface of the knife against the frosting. Repeat until the frosting is smooth.

6 Smooth the top with a hot palette knife, turning the cake with the flat surface of the knife against the frosting. Move the knife around the cake. Set for 15 minutes, then use a scraper to smooth the frosting all over the cake.

Red velvet cupcakes

These pretty red cupcakes are made from a light sponge cake topped with cream cheese frosting. The vinegar reacts with the baking soda, helping the cupcakes rise.

See page 46 for how to pipe.

20 mins prep

25 mins baking, plus cooling

Makes 12

For the cupcakes:

- 1 cup all-purpose flour
- 1 tbsp cocoa powder, sifted
- ½ tsp baking soda
- 1 tsp baking powder
- 7 tbsp unsalted butter, softened
- ½ cup sugar
- 1 tsp vanilla extract
- 1 tbsp red gel food coloring
- 1 large egg, beaten
- ½ cup buttermilk
- ½ tsp distilled white vinegar
- red or chocolate cake sprinkles, to decorate

For the frosting:

- 8 tbsp unsalted butter, softened
- 4oz (100g) cream cheese
- 2½ cups powdered sugar, sifted
- 1 tsp lemon juice

Special equipment:

- 12-hole muffin pan lined with 12 paper cupcake liners
- piping bag and star-shaped nozzle

1 Preheat the oven to 325°F (160°C). Put the flour, cocoa, baking soda, and baking powder in a bowl and stir to combine.

2 Put the butter and sugar in another bowl and beat with an electric mixer until light and fluffy. Beat in the vanilla extract and food coloring.

3 Beat in the egg together with 1 tbsp of the flour mixture, then alternately stir in the buttermilk and remaining flour mixture. Mix in the vinegar.

4 Divide the mixture evenly in the paper liners and bake in the oven for 25 minutes, until springy to the touch. Cool, then place on a wire rack.

Make the frosting

Add the sprinkles.

5 Beat the butter and cream cheese in a bowl with an electric mixer, then beat in the powdered sugar. Add the lemon juice and beat until paler. Pipe (see page 46) on top of each cupcake.

Vanilla cupcakes

Simple vanilla cupcakes are ideal for a birthday party or family get-together. Try the chocolate variation, too (see instructions to the right).

20 mins prep

15–20 mins baking, plus cooling

Makes 10

For the cupcakes:

- 1 cup self-rising flour
- 8 tbsp unsalted butter, softened
- ½ cup sugar
- 2 eggs, beaten
- 1 tsp vanilla extract

- 2 tbsp milk
- cake sprinkles, to decorate

For the frosting:

- 7 tbsp unsalted butter, softened
- 4oz (100g) cream cheese
- 2½ cups powdered sugar, sifted
- 1 tsp vanilla extract
- ½ tsp milk

Special equipment:

- 12-hole muffin pan lined with 10 paper cupcake liners

Chocolate cupcakes

Follow steps 1–2 for vanilla cupcakes, replacing ¼ cup of the flour for ¼ cup sifted cocoa powder. Then follow steps 3–4, replacing ¼ cup of the powdered sugar with cocoa powder to make chocolate frosting. Top with small pieces of freeze-dried raspberries.

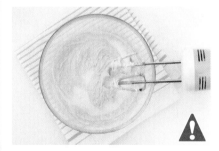

1 Preheat the oven to 350°F (180°C). Beat the flour, butter, sugar, eggs, and vanilla extract in a bowl, until combined. Then beat in the milk.

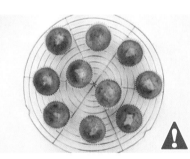

2 Fill the liners and bake for 15–20 minutes, until springy to the touch. Carefully remove from the oven, allow to cool, then place on a wire rack.

Make the frosting

3 Beat the butter and cream cheese in a bowl, then gradually beat in the powdered sugar. Beat in the vanilla extract and milk.

4 Pipe (see page 46) the buttercream on top of each cooled cupcake and decorate with your favorite sprinkles.

Choose pretty liners

Making chocolate

Chocolate and cocoa powder are made from the beans of the cacao tree. Here's how a small, bitter bean can be turned into a delicious cake flavoring.

1 GROWING

Cacao trees grow in hot, rainy tropical areas close to the equator. They thrive in the shade of taller trees, where they can get all the moisture they need but are protected from the hot sun.

Each tree produces around 30 seed pods. Cacao pods are shaped like footballs.

It's thought that British traders misspelled the word "cacao" when they brought the beans home, which is why we say "cocoa" instead.

Nearly 70 percent of the world's cacao trees grow in Africa. Ghana and Ivory Coast are the top producers of cocoa in the world.

5 ROASTING

At the factory, the dried beans are roasted inside huge ovens to develop more aroma and flavor. The roasting time varies, depending on the type of bean or the exact flavor the producers want to create.

After roasting, the beans are cooled before the next part of the process.

6 CRUSHING AND WINNOWING

Next, a big machine crushes the beans to remove the shells (husks), leaving the insides, which are called the nibs. The machine blasts the nibs with air to remove any last bits of the shell. This is called "winnowing."

The shells and nibs come out of different parts of the machine. Some bits of shell may be removed by hand, to make sure the chocolate is perfect.

Shell (husk)

Nibs

The paste is called cocoa mass.

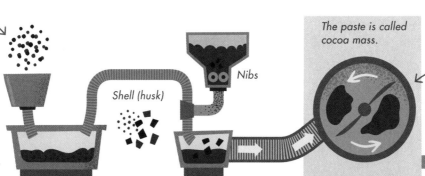

7 GRINDING

Next, the nibs are ground down to make a thick paste called cocoa mass or cocoa liquor. This can take a few hours.

Cocoa mass is made up of cocoa solids, which are pure, dry, unsweetened chocolate, and cocoa butter, the fatty part of the bean.

2 HARVESTING

Cacao pods turn yellow when they are ripe. The ripe pods are harvested (usually by hand) and cut open to reveal the seeds (beans) and pulp inside.

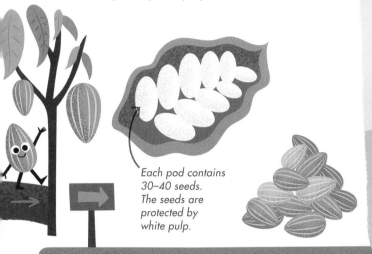

Each pod contains 30–40 seeds. The seeds are protected by white pulp.

3 FERMENTING AND DRYING

The farmers scoop out the wet cacao beans and pulp and pile them up. Over about a week, the pulp "sweats" in the heat and begins to ferment (a chemical reaction takes place). After fermenting, the beans are spread out in the sun to dry completely. This takes about a week, too.

The wet cacao beans "sweat."

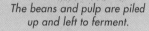

The beans and pulp are piled up and left to ferment.

The color of the beans gets darker as they dry.

4 ON THE MOVE

When the beans are dry, they are quality checked, sorted, then bagged and taken to a chocolate factory.

Yeah!

Let's go and become chocolate!

8 COCOA POWDER

To make cocoa powder, the cocoa mass is pressed to squeeze out most of the cocoa butter. The compressed roasted bean particles that remain are ground to a very fine powder.

Cocoa powder

Cocoa powder may be used in its pure form or have other ingredients added to give it a less bitter flavor.

Ready to be packaged.

9 CONCHING AND TEMPERING

To make solid chocolate, other ingredients, such as sugar and milk, need to be added to the cocoa mass. The mixture is heated and churned (this is called "conching") for a few hours to a few days. It's then heated and cooled progressively (this is called "tempering") to make it glossy and stable enough to be poured into molds, where it cools and hardens.

Finished chocolate

White chocolate doesn't contain any cocoa solids, so technically it's not really chocolate!

Hazelnut cake

Tasty hazelnuts give this cake an amazing flavor. If you can't find hazelnut flour (or meal) at the grocery store, buy whole shelled hazelnuts and grind them in a food processor.

20 mins prep | 60–65 mins baking, plus cooling | Serves 12

For the cake:

- 16 tbsp unsalted butter, softened, plus extra for greasing
- 1 cup sugar
- 4 eggs, separated
- ½ tsp almond extract
- 1¾ cups all-purpose flour
- 2 tsp baking powder
- 1 tsp salt
- ½ tsp baking soda
- ½ cup milk
- 2 cups hazelnut flour

Special equipment:

- 9in (23cm) loaf pan

Hazelnuts

1 Preheat the oven to 350°F (180°C). Grease the bottom and sides of the pan and line the bottom with parchment paper.

2 Put the butter and sugar in a large bowl and beat with an electric mixer until light and fluffy. Beat in the egg yolks one at a time, until fully combined. Beat in the almond extract.

3 In a medium-sized bowl, mix the flour, baking powder, salt, and baking soda, then gradually fold into the egg mixture, alternating with the milk. Fold in the hazelnut flour.

4 Place the egg whites in a large clean bowl and beat with an electric mixer or food processor until they form stiff peaks.

5 Fold a third of the egg whites into the hazelnut mixture to loosen it, then gently fold in the rest, until combined. Spoon into the pan and level out.

6 Bake for 60–65 minutes, or until a skewer inserted into the center comes out clean. Carefully cover with foil after 45 minutes to keep the top from burning.

Chocolate, orange, and hazelnut cake

For a chocolate chip and orange hazelnut cake, in step 2, cream together the butter and sugar with the finely grated zest of 1 orange. In step 2, replace the almond extract with 2 tablespoons of fresh orange juice. In step 3, stir in ¾ cup dark chocolate chips with the hazelnuts.

7 Carefully remove from the oven. Place on a wire rack. Cool in the pan for 15 minutes, then turn the cake onto the rack and peel off the paper.

Inside the bakery

Bakeries sell hundreds of cakes every day, so professional bakers need to be very fast and very organized. Big machines help speed up the processes and huge ovens can bake lots of cakes at the same time. Let's find out more...

1 INSIDE THE KITCHEN

The processes in a bakery are the same as the ones you do at home when you bake, just on a much larger scale.

The kitchen must be spotlessly clean.

Bakers often start work very early in the morning so that some cakes will be ready for customers when the store opens.

7 OTHER ELEMENTS

While the cakes are baking, the bakers might start on the next batch of cakes, or prepare fillings, frosting, or decorations for the cake.

6 BAKING

The huge ovens can fit lots of cakes in at the same time, but the cakes still need to be baked in batches. Timing is very important.

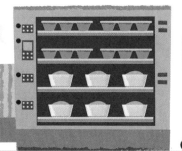

8 COOLING

When the cakes are perfectly baked, they are taken out of the oven and left to cool completely.

If you try to decorate a cake when it's still warm, the decoration may melt or slide off.

9 ASSEMBLING AND DECORATING

When the cakes are completely cool, they can be assembled and decorated. Layers may be added to create lots of different textures and flavors.

The decorations can be very tricky and intricate.

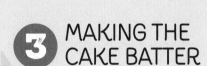

② PREPARATION

Being organized and well prepared is vital in a bakery. Before they start, the bakers plan their time and get all their ingredients and equipment ready.

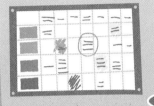

Cakes are prepared in batches, depending on how many will fit in the oven.

The bakers weigh the ingedients they need before they start, to save time.

③ MAKING THE CAKE BATTER

Depending on the recipe, different ingredients will need to be melted, mixed, beaten, whisked, sifted, folded, or stirred.

Bakers use big machines, like this stand mixer, which mixes quickly and can handle large amounts of batter.

⑤ POURING AND BRUSHING

The finished batter needs to be poured into pans or molds. The bakers make sure that all the cakes are the same size and the tops are level.

As with home baking, the pans need to be greased and/or lined first.

④ CHILLING AND SETTING

Some elements, such as mousses or jams, need to be made at the same time as the batter (or earlier) so they have time to chill or set before they are added to the baked cake.

Professional bakers often have to do a few things at the same time!

⑩ FINISHED PRODUCT

The fresh, beautifully decorated cakes are usually displayed in the store window or behind a glass counter. Who can resist?

Most cakes will be sold in the bakery, but some may be sent to other stores and cafés.

Pound cake

Pound cake dates back to the 1700s, when the recipe used a pound each of four ingredients: flour, butter, sugar, and eggs. The recipe makes a deliciously moist and buttery cake.

This cake bakes best in a loaf pan.

10 mins prep

40–45 mins baking, plus cooling

Serves 8–10

For the cake:

- 15 tbsp unsalted butter, softened, plus extra for greasing
- 1 cup sugar
- 2 tsp vanilla extract
- 3 eggs, beaten
- 1½ cups self-rising flour
- 1 tsp baking powder
- 3 tbsp milk

Special equipment:

- 9in (23cm) loaf pan

Baking powder

Flour

1 Preheat the oven to 350°F (180°C). Grease the bottom and sides of the pan and line with parchment paper.

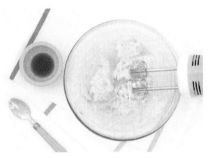

2 Put the butter and sugar in a bowl and beat with an electric mixer until light and fluffy, then beat in the vanilla extract.

3 Add the eggs, a little at a time, beating well after each addition.

4 Combine the flour and baking powder, then fold them into the wet mixture using a large spoon. Stir in the milk.

5 Transfer the mixture to the pan and smooth the top using the back of a spoon. Bake in the oven for 40–45 minutes, or until risen and golden and a skewer inserted in the center comes out clean.

6 Remove from the oven and place on a wire rack. Let cool in the pan for 10 minutes, then remove from the pan, peel off the parchment paper, and place on the rack to cool.

← Carefully cut into slices to serve.

Serve with a glass of milk.

Strawberry glaze cake

This delicious cake is baked in a special pan with a raised bottom. When the cake is turned out of the pan, the hollow inside is perfect for all kinds of fruit. A flan pan with a raised bottom works, too.

20 mins prep | 25–30 mins baking, plus cooling | Serves 10–12

For the cake:

- butter, for greasing
- 3 eggs, separated
- 1 tbsp cold water
- ¾ cup sugar
- 2 tsp vanilla sugar (optional)
- 1¼ cups all-purpose flour
- ½ tsp baking powder
- whipped cream, to serve

For the filling and glaze:

- 12oz (400g) fresh strawberries, hulled and halved
- 3oz (85g) package strawberry geletin
- ½ cup sugar
- 3 tbsp cornstarch
- 1 cup water

Special equipment:

- 11in (28cm) tart pan with a raised bottom or a flan pan

1 Preheat the oven to 350°F (180°C). Generously grease the pan with butter.

2 Put the egg whites and cold water in a large clean bowl and beat with an electric mixer until foamy and doubled in size.

3 Gradually beat in the sugar a little at a time, beating well after each addition, until the mixture is thick and shiny. Beat in the vanilla sugar, if using.

4 Beat the egg yolks together and fold them into the mixture, then gently sift the flour and baking powder into the mixture and fold in.

Serve with a dollop of whipped cream.

Strawberries are especially pretty cut lengthwise from top to bottom

5 Spoon the mixture into the pan, level the top, then tap the pan gently on the work surface to remove air bubbles.

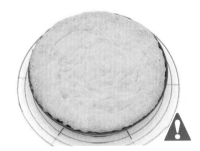

6 Bake in the oven for 25–30 minutes, or until risen and golden and firm to the touch. Carefully remove from the oven.

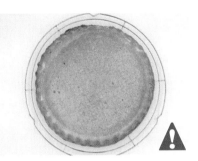

7 Cool in the pan for 5 minutes, then turn onto a wire rack to cool.

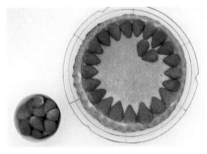

8 Arrange the strawberries cut-side down over the bottom of the cooled cake, starting from the outside edge and finishing at the center.

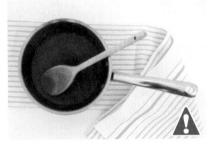

9 Combine the strawberry gelatin, sugar, cornstarch, and water in small pan. Bring to a boil over medium heat, stirring frequently. Cook at a rapid boil for 1 minute, stirring constantly, until thickened. Let cool for 15 minutes.

10 Carefully spoon the glaze mixture over the fruit and in between the gaps. Allow to set.

Make this cake when strawberries are in season.

Cake in numbers

By now you know a lot about how to make some amazing cakes, and where your ingredients come from. But here are some facts that you probably don't know, from the history of cakes to some record-breaking, one-time creations.

SOME OF THE EARLIEST "CAKES" WERE ACTUALLY DISKS OF GRAIN THAT HAD BEEN DRIED AND COMPACTED TOGETHER.

The ancient Egyptians probably invented cake, around **5,000** years ago. Their honey-sweetened breads were pretty cakey.

Baking powder and baking soda became baking staples in the 1800s, making it much easier to create light, airy cakes.

The oldest known cake in the world is more than 4,000 years old. It was sealed in an ancient Egyptian grave in around 2200 BCE.

The word "cake" comes from the old Norse word "kaka." The word is still used for cake in Icelandic and Swedish.

70% of all cakes sold in Swedish bakeries are "princess cakes," made from a recipe inspired by the Swedish royal family.

The longest cake ever was 17,388 ft (5,300 m) long and baked in Kerala,

Cupcakes were invented in the US in the **19TH CENTURY** and got their name because the ingredients were measured with and then baked in cups.

In the 16th century, the Italians swapped yeast for beaten eggs to make their cakes lighter.

The tallest cake was **108¼ ft (33 m)** tall, about the same as six giraffes standing on top of each other. The cake was made for a Christmas exhibition in Indonesia in 2008.

The world's most expensive cake cost **$75 MILLION.** It was 6 ft (1.8 m) long and decorated with 4,000 real diamonds.

Before the wire whisk was invented in the 19th century, people used bundles of twigs to whisk their cake batter!

The earliest English-language recipe for a sponge cake comes from a 1615 book by an English poet, Gervase Markham.

FROSTING USED TO BE SPREAD ON CAKES WITH A FEATHER.

The first tiered wedding cake was made for the wedding of Queen Victoria's eldest daughter in 1858.

People eat between **50 and 100 million** birthday cakes around the world every day.

India, in 2020. It took the crowd only 10 minutes to eat it!

Glossary

BATCH
Making or baking things in more than one time, usually if you do not have enough pans or space in the oven.

BEAT
Stirring or mixing ingredients quickly until smooth, using a whisk, spoon, or electric mixer.

CARBON DIOXIDE
A colorless gas that's responsible for the "rise" in baked goods.

CHURN
Moving something vigorously in a machine, such as milk or cream, to make butter.

COMBINE
Mixing ingredients together evenly.

CRYSTALLIZATION
The process of forming crystals.

DRIZZLE
Pouring liquid slowly in a thin trickle.

DUST
Lightly sprinkling a fine layer of powdered food, such as sugar, on top of a cake.

EQUATOR
An imaginary horizontal line that runs around the middle of Earth.

EVAPORATE
Using heat to remove liquid.

FERMENT
Converting carbohydrates into yeast or alcohol.

FLOUR
A fine powder made by grinding up edible grains.

FOLD
Mixing ingredients together gently, to keep as much air in the mixture as possible.

GLUTEN
A protein found in wheat, rye, and barley grains.

GREASE
Rubbing butter or oil onto a baking sheet or pan to stop food from sticking to it.

HULLED
Having the hull or husk removed from a grain or a fruit, such as a strawberry.

LEAVENING
To make food gain air bubbles by adding a rising (leavening) agent, such as baking powder or baking soda.

LINE
Placing parchment paper or foil in a pan so that food won't stick to it.

MACERATE
Leaving fruit on sugar to soften it and release the juices from the fruit.

PREHEAT
To make an oven hot, ready for baking an item of food, such as a cake.

PURIFY
To make an ingredient clean or pure.

RISE
Cake gets bigger in size when baked.

ROAST
To cook food in the oven at a high temperature.

SIFT
Using a sieve to remove lumps from dry ingredients.

SIMMER
Cooking over low heat, so the mixture in the pan is bubbling gently but not boiling.

SPRINGFORM
A round pan with a latch on the side.

TEXTURE
The way something looks and feels, e.g., soft, smooth, chunky, or moist.

TURN ONTO
Taking food out of a pan or sheet and carefully laying it on a surface.